FIFTY YEARS AGO

At Home

Karen Bryant-Mole

WAYLAND

Titles in the series
At Home
Going on a Trip
Having Fun
In the High Street

find Wayland on the Internet at http://www.wayland.co.uk

All Wayland books encourage children to read and help them improve their literacy.

 The contents page, page numbers, headings and index help locate specific pieces of information.

 The glossary reinforces alphabetic knowledge and extends vocabulary.

 The further information section suggests other books dealing with the same subject.

 Find out more about how this book is specifically relevant to the National Literacy Strategy on page 31.

Editor: Carron Brown
Consultant: Norah Granger
Cover design: White Design
Inside design: Michael Leaman
Photo stylist: Gina Brown
Production controller: Carol Titchener

First published in 1998 by
Wayland Publishers Limited,
61 Western Road, Hove,
East Sussex BN3 1JD

Typeset in England by Michael Leaman
Printed and bound in Italy by L.G. Canale &
C.S.p.A, Turin

British Library Cataloguing in Publication Data
Bryant-Mole, Karen
    At home. – (Fifty years ago)   1. Family –
    Great Britain – History – 20th century –
    Juvenile literature. 2. Great Britain Social
    conditions – 1945 – Juvenile literature.
    3. Great Britain – Social life and customs –
    1945 – Juvenile literature.
    I. Title 941'. 085

ISBN 0 7502 23936

Picture acknowledgements
The publishers would like to thank
the following for allowing their pictures
to be used in this book: Corbis 9, 25;
Getty Images *cover* [main] 5, 7, 11, 21; Robert
Harding 13, 17; Topham 15, 19, 23, 27; Wayland
Picture Library/Angela Hampton *cover* [inset], 4,
5, 6, 7, 8, 10, 11, 12, 14, 16, 18, 20, 22, 24, 26.

CONTENTS

In this book we are introduced to the Taylor family. We will meet Mr and Mrs Taylor, their children Luke and Sophie, and Luke and Sophie's grandparents Stan and Maureen. Compare their life at home today to family life at home fifty years ago.

WASHING CLOTHES

This washing machine fills itself with water.

Mr Taylor will add the washing powder, choose the wash programme he wants to use and then press the start button. When the clothes are washed, the machine will spin out most of the water.

This woman's washing machine was filled with water from a tap.

Few people had washing machines fifty years ago. They had to wash everything by hand. When they had washed their clothes they put them through a mangle to squeeze out the water.

I remember...

Maureen Taylor is Luke and Sophie's grandmother. She remembers the wash days in her house. 'My mum used to keep her washing machine in a cupboard. It had little wheels underneath it. When she wanted to use it, she pushed it over to the sink. You had to push the clothes around by hand.'

Mrs Taylor is pouring water into her steam iron.

Mrs Taylor can choose whether she wants her iron to be hot or cool. She uses different temperatures for different types of material. She uses steam to help get any creases out of the clothes. The Taylor family have some clothes that do not need to be ironed.

This woman used a dry iron.

It was quite difficult to get creases out of clothes with an iron like this. It was easier to iron clothes when they were slightly damp. Fifty years ago, almost all clothes had to be ironed.

I remember...

Stan remembers his mum hanging out the washing on a clothes line in the yard. 'My mum said the wind blew most of the creases out and made the clothes easier to iron. After the clothes were ironed, she hung them on a clothes horse which she stood in front of the coal fire, to let the clothes air.'

COOKING

Mr Taylor is putting a ready-prepared meal into the microwave.

Mr Taylor sometimes has to work quite late. If he wants a meal in a hurry, he takes some food out of the freezer and cooks it in the microwave. The Taylors also use an electric cooker for cooking.

This little girl helped her mum with the cooking.

Fifty years ago, there was a shortage of some kinds food. This was because of the Second World War which had ended in 1945. Many kinds of food were very expensive, so people did a lot of baking at home.

I remember...

Maureen remembers helping her mum in the kitchen. 'I learned everything I know about cooking from my mum. She also taught me not to waste food. Left-over meat would be minced up and made into pies. Bones would be boiled and the liquid used for soup. It was always mum who did the cooking.'

Luke and Sophie usually have their tea before their dad gets home from work.

Luke and Sophie are having pizza at tea-time. Pizza is Sophie's favourite meal. Luke prefers pasta with a chicken sauce.

This family ate Sunday dinner together.

Fifty years ago, it was more usual for a family to have a meal together than it is today. In the past, people usually lived much nearer their work and got home earlier.

I remember...

Stan Taylor is Luke and Sophie's grandfather. His dad was a coal miner. 'My dad worked shifts. If he was home, we all ate together. If he was working, it was just mum who ate with us. Sunday dinner was the most important meal of the week. We always ate together on Sundays.'

STORING FOOD

Sophie is putting a loaf of bread into the freezer.

Mr and Mrs Taylor go to the supermarket once a week to buy food. They store tins and packets in the kitchen cupboards. Foods such as milk, cheese and cold meats are kept in the fridge. Anything they want to keep for a long time is stored in the freezer.

These people look very proud of their new fridge.

Today, almost everyone has a fridge in their home. Fifty years ago, fridges were very expensive. Anyone who had a fridge was thought to be very lucky.

I remember...

There was no fridge in Maureen's home when she was a child. 'We kept our food in a sort of walk-in cupboard, called a larder. There was wire mesh netting on the windows to stop insects flying in. In summer, we stood our bottles of milk in buckets of cold water. But I still remember the horrible taste of warm milk.'

WASHING UP

Luke is loading the dishwasher.

Tea is over and Luke is helping to clear up. The Taylor family have a dishwasher. Luke puts the dirty cups and glasses in the top rack. He places the dirty plates, knives and forks on the bottom rack.

These girls did their washing up by hand.

No one had a dishwasher in their house fifty years ago. These girls washed their dishes in the sink. When the dishes were clean, they placed them on a draining board and then dried them with a tea towel.

I remember...

When Maureen was growing up, there was no running hot water in their house. 'I remember as a little girl helping my mother wash the dishes in an old stoneware sink. The dishes drained on a wooden drainer. My mother had to heat the water in a kettle and then carry it to the sink.'

KEEPING WARM

The Taylors have radiators in every room.

Even when it's cold outside, the Taylors are warm inside their house. Hot water flows through the radiators, warming up the air in the rooms. The water is heated by a gas-fired boiler. An electric pump pushes the water round the radiators.

This family had a coal fire in their living room.

Fifty years ago, most homes had coal fires. Gas fires and electric heaters were becoming popular. They were less work than coal fires and cleaner too. They could be turned on and off quickly.

I remember...

Stan only had coal fires in his house. 'It was my job to bring in the coal from the coalhouse in the yard. Every morning, my mum swept out the ashes from the day before and I laid a new fire. We had no heating upstairs. In winter, my bedroom was freezing. I remember finding frost on the inside of my bedroom windows.'

Luke is cleaning the floor of his bedroom with a vacuum cleaner.

Sophie and Luke tidy and clean their own bedrooms. Mrs Taylor does most of the rest of the housework. The floors and work surfaces we have today are easy to keep clean.

This woman had to clean around her fireplace by hand.

Fifty years ago, coal fires made everything very dusty and dirty. Dusting and polishing took a long time. Some people had vacuum cleaners. Other people used a carpet sweeper or swept the carpet with a brush.

I remember...

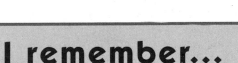

Stan remembers how his mum cleaned the carpet. 'She used to sprinkle damp tea leaves on the floor and then sweep them up with a dustpan and brush! She said it kept the dust down. Every spring, she did her spring cleaning. Each room was emptied, everything was washed or cleaned and polished and then it was all put back again.'

ENTERTAINMENT

The Taylors are watching a video on their television set.

The Taylors all enjoy watching television. If they go out, they can video programmes and watch them later. Sometimes, they hire videos from the video library. If they want to hear music, they listen to the radio or play CDs.

FIFTY YEARS AGO

This family is getting ready to listen to a radio programme.

Fifty years ago, few people had television sets but almost every family had a radio. There were only three radio stations. People also liked to listen to records on a gramophone.

I remember...

Stan's favourite radio programme was called Children's Hour. 'You always learned something new when you tuned in to Children's Hour. It was interesting but it was fun, too. Fifty years ago, all the programmes were broadcast by the BBC. Today there is much more choice.'

PLAYING INDOORS

Luke and Sophie like playing games together on the computer.

Sophie enjoys adventure games on the computer. Luke prefers car-racing games. They also use the computer to chat with friends around the world on the Internet.

FIFTY YEARS AGO

Family board games were very popular fifty years ago.

This family is playing a board game. Few families had a television set, so games were a good way for the whole family to have fun together. There were no home computers fifty years ago.

I remember...

Stan's favourite toy was a clockwork train set. 'I used to lay the set out on my bedroom floor and run the track under my bed. When the train disappeared under the bed, I pretended it was in a tunnel. I also had a stamp collection. I saved up my pocket money to buy packets of stamps from around the world.'